WHAT DOGS TEACH US II

What Dogs Teach Us II

More! LIFE'S LESSONS LEARNED FROM OUR BEST FRIENDS

GLENN DROMGOOLE

WILLOW CREEK PRESS

Remembering Pola and Honey, who were my teachers.

Published by Willow Creek Press
P.O. Box 147, Minocqua, Wisconsin 54548

Photo Credits: John Daniels/ardea.com: 8, 23, 35, 44, 51, 65, 82, 84, 87, 90;
Rolf Kopfle/ardea.com: 22; Jean Michel Labat/ardea.com: 39, 93;
Johan De Meester/ardea.com: 9; BIOS/Peter Arnold, Inc.: 73;
Biosphoto/Thiriet Claudius/Peter Arnold Inc.: 38; Mike Maloney/Peter Arnold, Inc.: 36;
WILDLIFE/Peter Arnold, Inc.: 7; Denver Bryan/Images on the Wildside: 24, 48, 49, 50, 69;
John Eriksson/Images on the Wildside: 53; Sam Allen/KimballStock.com: 61;
Close Encounters of the Furry Kind/KimballStock.com: 13, 46, 79;
Ron Kimball/KimballStock.com: 12, 15, 21, 25, 33, 45, 47, 74, 76, 78, 80, 81, 86, 89;
Mark McQueen/KimballStock.com: 2, 60; Gary Randall Photography/KimballStock.com:
41; Martin Rogers/KimballStock.com: 31; Richard Stacks/KimballStock.com: 34;
Renee Stockdale/KimballStock.com: 52; age fotostock/SuperStock: 10, 14, 17, 18, 63, 64,
70, 88, 94, 95; Francisco Cruz/SuperStock: 27; Fogstock LLC/SuperStock: 16;
Geri Lavrov/SuperStock: 66; Mauritius/SuperStock: 11; George Ostertag/SuperStock: 75;
Prisma/SuperStock: 85; Super Stock Inc./SuperStock: 40, 92; Yoshio Tomii/SuperStock: 42

Editor: Andrea Donner
Printed in Canada

Contents

About Getting
Along With Others

K now who
your friends are.

Make new friends along the way.

Keep your nose out of someone else's business.

Listen to
what others
have to say...

Even when
they can be a
little annoying.

It always helps to say please.

Try to live in harmony with one another.

*S*ometimes you
need to speak
your mind...

At other times, it's best to keep your thoughts to yourself.

Learn how to keep a secret.

E njoy spending time together.

Let people know you like them.

Stay close to your pals.

Do something nice for someone you love.

Bring out the best in others.

Teamwork

is important.

A kiss helps
patch things up.

Praise more; criticize less.

A smile makes everyone feel a little better.

I f you're kind, it will show in your eyes.

There's no time like the present to let

a friend know you care.

*S*avor a quiet moment with someone special.

F ads come and go, but friends are forever.

About Self-Respect

Never, never, never give up.

D on't let
anyone take away
your dignity.

There's so much to learn.

Keep your eye on the ball.

T ake pride
in who you are.

W_e all
have a touch of
royalty in us...

But loyalty trumps royalty in our book.

Don't quit until the job is done..

Keep your ears open;
you might learn something new.

Some days
you just feel like
growling...

But you don't want to stay that way for too long.

Pay attention to your appearance.

Add a touch of color to your life.

K eep your
cool at all times.

There is
such a thing as
"too cute."

Don't let obstacles get in your way.

Y ou don't have to roll over
just because someone says to.

y ou can learn a lot if you keep quiet and listen.

Develop a firm handshake.

Keep your eyes open for opportunities.

Get your

licks in while

you can.

Treat yourself to a new toy every once in a while.

T ake the plunge and make the most of it.

About Health & Fitness

Start the day with a good breakfast.

Make sure your diet includes plenty of fruits...

And vegetables.

Run for your life!

Jump for joy!

Drink plenty of water every day.

Contentment

is a great gift.

It's hard to get
in trouble when
you're asleep.

A walk is good for the heart and the soul.

A good day off beats a good day at work.

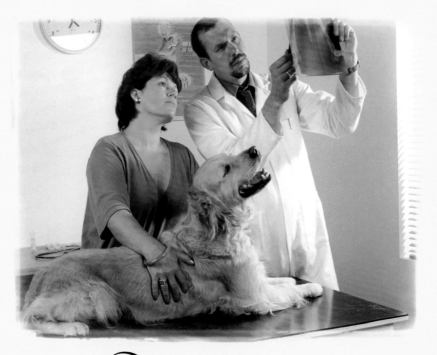

Get an annual physical exam.

All babies need tender loving care.

T urn off the TV and let's play!

Remember where you put things.

Know how to find your way home.

Get out and stretch your legs.

Find time in your busy schedule for a nap.

About a Better Life

It would be a better world if we treated each other

as well as our dogs treat us.

Follow your heart.

Cherish the simple things in life.

K now when

it's time to leave.

Be a good
neighbor.

Good things come in small packages.

A pure heart is to be treasured.

Firemen are our friends.

Home is wherever the people you love are.

Wouldn't it be boring if we were all alike?

Dream big, really big.

Learn to appreciate the finer things in life.

Be aware of the beauty around you.

Make your own music.

Dance to your own rhythm.

Traveling is
more fun with
a friend.

Remember, mom usually knows best.

K eep up with the news.

J ust say
"Awwww!"

There are some things people just shouldn't try to do.

 T each young ones what they need to know.

N ever underestimate the power of a puppy.

Make a difference in someone's life.

Celebrate another day of living.